13 Life Le…

S. Dale McHenry

© Copyright 2016, S. Dale McHenry

ISBN: 978-1-973-55046-4

Contents

Prologue 1

The Setting: Philmont 5

1: Start 9

2: Teach 11

3: Lost 15

4: Distraction 19

5: Lift 23

6: Darkness 29

7: Solutions 33

8: Beauty 41

9: Difficulty 47

10: Milestones 53

11: Prepare 57

12: Risk 60

13: Luck 67

Coda 73

Prologue

We were deep into the back-country at the Philmont Scout Reservation in New Mexico.

It was late afternoon in a trail camp in the high Rocky Mountains: 45 degrees, windy, and hailing. Our trek crew of 9 Boy Scouts and 3 adult leaders was huddled around a very wet, smoky campfire that seemed to be violating the laws of chemistry by generating no discernible heat. I had donned every article of clothing and rain gear from my backpack, and I was <u>still</u> losing the battle with the cold. I was wearing wool socks as mittens. I was shivering, and my teeth were audibly chattering.

To a veteran Scouter, this might seem unremarkable or even routine. Except that it was mid July.

Two days earlier, we were struggling to stay hydrated in unbearable heat. But Thursday had dawned at 32 degrees. We had hiked through rain and hail for seven or eight miles of steeply climbing trail. We were wet and tired, and contemplating the prospects of tomorrow's steep climb over the top of a 12,000 foot peak with full backpacks. Afternoon thunderstorms were forecast. We mentally rehearsed our lightning training, which seemed to focus on dispersing the group widely enough so that when the lightning ceased, there would <u>probably</u> be enough survivors to attempt CPR on the less fortunate.

We had just taken on four days of food and had loaded up with two days of extra water, so our backpacks were the heaviest they'd ever been. Blisters and sore spots had been steadily accumulating, while Advil and Band-Aids were dwindling. Tomorrow was going to be tough. Really tough.

Our motivational bright spot for the march was that our destination campsite sported a black powder rifle range, one of the more sought after activities. Upon arrival, we discovered that the range was fully booked for the day. So much for fun.

During dinner, we had once again discovered a mysterious gap in our Oreo supplies. This had been going on for a few days, and we were all silently cycling through mental rosters of the crew members, laying odds on which of our group was a thief.

While preparing to hang our food bags on the bear line, a boy had hopelessly snarled both of our ropes on a tree limb forty feet over our heads. Bold experiments to untangle these ropes had proved completely fruitless, actually making the problem steadily worse. The boys were at each other's throats, working through the proper assignment of blame with the precision of neurosurgeons.

And the icing on the cake was that it was three days

to the next supply depot, and we were <u>critically</u> short of toilet paper.

Aside from the shivering and teeth chattering, I was, like a good Scout leader, calm and stoic on the outside. But my mind was a very dark place, full of thoughts that violated all twelve points of the Scout Law.

Again and again, I asked myself "Why am I here? Why would anyone want to do this a second time?"

The answers to these questions have gradually revealed themselves over the ensuing five years.

The Setting: Philmont

Philmont is a 214 square-mile Boy Scout reservation in Cimarron, New Mexico. It is located at the exact point where the seemingly endless Great Plains leap into the grandeur of the Rocky Mountains. Grasslands suddenly sprout alpine forests. We owe a great debt to Waite Phillips for donating this beautiful setting to the Boy Scouts of America.

Base Camp occupies the last patch of level ground at 7,200 feet elevation, and peaks of 9,000 to 12,000 feet lurk immediately to the west. When one steps off the bus, it takes little imagination to understand that adventure, rigor, and nature at her rawest lurk in your immediate future.

Base Camp contains impressive facilities to maintain an operation that each day launches 300 Scouters into the wilderness and monitors the progress of 3,000 as they move through the back country. It includes a medical facility run by the Kansas University School of Medicine, large stores of food & camping gear, and one of the most impressive retail outlets of outdoor gear in the nation. But this hub of civilized activity sits alone on the edge of a vast wilderness.

Beyond the confines of Base Camp, there exists just enough infrastructure to maintain minimal necessary levels of safety for a Scouting operation. Just barely.

There are 125 campsites scattered across this vast area. About 30 of them are staffed with a few intrepid rangers who live in Spartan cabins. Perhaps a half-dozen sites have stores of food and fuel to resupply hikers during their treks. But <u>most</u> campsites contain only a rudimentary privy, a few clearings for pitching tents, and <u>maybe</u> a source of untreated water. Along the miles of trails between these sites, you're on your own.

In the back-country, it's you against Mother Nature, and she's not always kind. Trails can be steep and rocky and seemingly endless. Wild animals and wilder weather lurk. During the middle of the summer, afternoon rain and hail storms are frequently punctuated with lightning.

Less than a dozen of these camps have basic shower facilities (with wood-fired water heaters), and our route passed only one of these over a period of twelve days. You may be surprised to learn that one can bathe only once a week in mid-summer and still be a functioning member of a social group. You can, **if** everyone else is doing likewise. For example, the sophisticated social and intellectual interactions that eventually led to the Italian Renaissance managed to occur in the late Middle Ages, a time when even the most hygienic of nobles exuded an olfactory miasma akin to that of the Kansas City stockyards. At the time, this was considered normal and unworthy of comment. So it was with us.

On our last morning in the back-country, we encountered a skunk on the trail. He turned up his nose in disgust and scampered off at a brisk pace. Normally, finding oneself at the pointy end of such elitism would have stung a bit, but our time on the trail had elevated us beyond the reach of such pretentiousness.

Two weeks in this environment took its toll on folks. In my first morning at Base Camp, I watched several crews coming down Tooth Ridge from their treks. Some were literally limping along in boots with split soles wrapped in duct tape. Others were struggling to carry damaged backpacks barely held together with cord and tape. A few dusty bandages peeked out of socks. Everyone was unkempt and grubby. But to a man, they all had a certain demeanor about them that intrigued me. They were battered, but not beaten. They had faced what will probably be the most physically challenging event of their lives, and they had won.

The people coming in to Base Camp after 12 days in the Philmont back-country are different than the people heading out. Most will treasure the experience for the rest of their lives and encourage Scouters all over the world to sign up for a Philmont trek.

If you ever get the chance to go to Philmont, do it.

What is so powerful about the experience? Why do people sign up? In a world full of comforts and distractions, Philmont has neither. Yet because of that, it is one of the most powerful learning environments most of us will ever encounter.

Here are some of those lessons.

1: Start

I didn't go to Philmont when I was a Scout. The Kansas City council had an excellent summer camp program in the Ozark Mountains, and that seemed to be more than enough for a small town boy from the flat part of the state.

As I became active as a leader in my son's troop in New Jersey, a couple of the other leaders wanted to introduce a high adventure program to help retain the older boys. One pressed us to form up a crew for Sea Base, a Scouting facility in the Florida Keys focused on ocean activities. I had never been sailing on the open ocean. I knew nothing about it. Sea Base provided a structured program to teach us how to live out of a boat for a week. It turned out to be a lot of fun, and the Scouts learned a lot about an aspect of Scouting that was completely new to us.

Other leaders said good things about Sea Base, but they were <u>absolutely effusive</u> about Philmont. Their enthusiasm was nearly unbounded. They encouraged us to take the next step on the High Adventure pathway and form a Philmont crew.

There were scores of reasons to <u>not</u> sign up. I knew that the rigors of hiking over one hundred miles at a high altitude would far eclipse the challenges of living on a small boat for a week. I was fifty two years old and was

<u>not</u> a physical fitness buff. It was two weeks away from the office in a busy part of the year. I didn't have any of the necessary equipment. And so on.

But our Council had a <u>very</u> thorough training program to get crews ready for the experience, complete with tons of advice and training about equipment, training hikes, logistics, etc. So that excuse went away.

The troop signed up for a crew slot of three adults and nine scouts. They were going to go, and they needed some leaders. None of our leaders had been to Philmont before. So although I knew next to nothing about wilderness backpacking, I signed up.

I had nagging concerns about my ability to tackle this job, but I couldn't let the boys down. At that point, I was committed, and I was going to Philmont unless I broke a leg getting ready.

It was one of the best decisions I've ever made in my life.

Lesson #1: Many people fail by not taking the first step.

2: Teach

Starting a year in advance, the training began. The first three months consisted of meetings to educate the three adults in the crew about the experience, the logistics, and the financial requirements. There was a lot of encouragement for adults to drop some weight and get in shape. The prospect of this trek motivated me to adopt a program of regular exercise that was entirely new to me. I have kept it up ever since. I owe a debt to Scouting for this.

A crew must learn a lot to function successfully at Philmont. When you get off the bus, a Training Ranger is assigned to the crew. The first day is a fire-hose dose of training courses covering scores of topics ranging across first aid, navigation, water purification, weather management, etc. For many crews, this is the extent of their preparation.

For a crew to be really ready, they need to spend a few months ahead of time cranking through basics. We signed up for CPR and Wilderness First Aid courses. We assigned specialties to crew members: water acquisition, cooking, medical, gear assessment, camp set-up, etc. We went shopping at outdoor stores for gear and slowly came to understand the weight versus benefits tradeoffs of the stuff in our backpacks.

We all watched many web-videos of best practices.

We invited Philmont veterans to speak to our crew.

And then we actually went out on dry run hikes. These were frustrating and enlightening. After hours of unsuccessful attempts at setting up bear bags, cooking stoves, and shelters, the boys gradually came to realize that they really did have to master their assigned skills.

Thankfully, it rained and snowed on one of our practice hikes. Two inches of snow were followed by a raging nor'easter. Wet clothes and deep chills drove home lessons about rain gear and layering that will last for a lifetime.

Another practice hike on a hot day with over-full packs drove home the importance of backpack weight management. Failure of straps and ties led to the assignment of a "maintenance specialist" in the crew.

It was hard to stand by and watch these failures unfold, but the school of hard knocks is the most effective academy. Lasting lessons are best taught by failures in managed risk situations. The art of being a parent is to give children room to make mistakes and learn from them. Our job isn't to <u>prevent</u> mistakes, but to carefully catalyze them, with intervention aimed at preventing the mistakes from having unrecoverable consequences. We were fortunate in that most of our worst backpacking mistakes were made close to home, well in advance of stepping off the bus at Philmont.

Sometimes when failure might lead to physical injury, alternatives to the fail & learn strategy must be found. The most effective staffers at Philmont have cracked the code on safety lessons. Whether the lesson was spar-pole climbing at Crater Lake or horse-riding at Beaubien, many safety lessons ended in the simple phrase "...and if you don't do it that way, you're gonna die." It held the audience's attention, and <u>not</u> getting the lesson across wasn't an option.

LESSON #2: Teachers have hard jobs.

3: Lost

One of the assigned roles in our crew was "navigator". This individual was responsible for the compass, maps, and GPS unit. At the beginning of each day, he selected our route, and at each fork in the trail, he was to determine the correct path to take.

We all know someone whose confidence far exceeds their capability. They purport to know everything about a particular topic, tout their expertise at every available opportunity, jealously guard access to key information, and dominate deliberations on "their" topic. At the beginning of our journey, our navigator was one of those people. Nobody else was allowed access to the maps and compass.

On the first day of our trek, we were dropped off on poorly blazed "feeder trails", and our first mission was to find the main trail. Our navigator took command. After an hour or two, we had returned to the same starting point twice. Our navigator's confidence had not been shaken a bit. He remained "100% confident" on the third attempt, only to yet again return to our original starting point. He then loudly announced that the maps were incorrect and that the compass was obviously defective.

The circumstances that doomed Amelia Earhart were starting to become apparent in our group. But as leaders, we were sworn to let the boys work it out on their own. Friction was building to uncomfortable levels. Fortunately, another crew eventually passed by and loudly proclaimed the correct way to the main trail. After several seconds of tinkering with his instruments, the navigator mysteriously settled on the same bearing taken by the other crew, and we found the main trail 15 minutes later.

The same proceedings unfolded the very next morning, almost in the shadow of a large signpost with a prominent arrow pointing at the trail to our intended mountain pass. The navigator proclaimed the sign to be "wrong" and lobbied vigorously for us to take a cow path leading to a distant pasture. A protracted process ensued that resembled that of a criminal trial jury with a sole dissenting member.

George Will has observed that American football embraces the worst aspects of our national character: sporadic violence punctuated by interminable committee meetings. We had fully embraced the latter, and were teetering on the brink of sliding into the former.

After seemingly hours of patient negotiation, the main part of the crew opted for an alternative approach: they just strapped on their packs and trudged up the clearly marked trail. Sensing that he was espousing a lost cause, the navigator begrudgingly joined in at the rear of the line.

Our navigator never did see fit to consult with any of his peers, but after a few days, he would sometimes discretely consult one of the adults when he was disoriented. He had learned a key lesson: admitting what you don't know is less embarrassing than failure.

<u>LESSON #3: Place learning ahead of ego. Asking for help and advice is a sign of maturity. Do it often.</u>

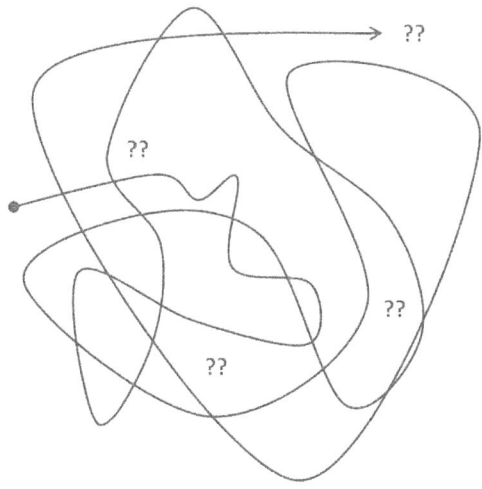

4: Distraction

Scouting is a program designed to build character, and the chief catalyst of character-building is discomfort.

Any veteran scouter has a pantheon of stories about bad food, fatigue, sunburn, swarms of biting bugs, wet gear, and thousands of other problems. In fact, the program is specifically <u>designed</u> to ensure that most of these miseries befall each and every scout.

Eventually, every Scout learns an important lesson: When the food is bad, the weather is miserable, the bugs are biting, and there are five more miles to hike, complaining doesn't make it go faster or better. In fact, it's the opposite. So don't complain. Tough it out and prepare better the next time.

Philmont takes this normal set of challenges and trebles it. Right out of the gate, the challenge is hiking up huge hills with 50 pounds on your back in thin mountain air. Heroes last about 5 minutes in this setting.

Our training included a procedure called "caterpillaring". Here's how it works: As the crew line progresses up a steep trail, about every 20 yards, the front man steps to the side of the trail to let the rest of the crew pass. He then joins in at the back of the line. So the crew progresses much like the tread on a bulldozer. The effect is to introduce a 30 second opportunity to catch one's breath every two minutes or so. That makes a HUGE difference. The crew can proceed steadily with minimal full stops.

Caterpillaring made the climbs physically tolerable, but they were still tough. On one particularly strenuous day, we stumbled upon an interesting pursuit while we were caterpillaring up hill after hill. Each resting man posed a two-choice question to each passing crew member. "Yankees or Mets?" "Dogs or cats?" "Brussels sprouts or spinach?" "Superman or Batman?"

The Gallup Poll folks would have been proud of all the information we gathered over a three-hour segment of our hike. Each man spent most of his time thinking up increasingly clever questions to ask. And let me assure you, there were some mighty clever, multi-layered choices presented, the majority of them in reasonably good taste. The time passed quickly, and we showed remarkably little fatigue as we finally rolled into our next camp.

We had discovered the value of mental distraction. Sometimes focus isn't a good thing, especially when it's on the negative. When you're doing something physically demanding, think about something else other than your sore legs, gasping lungs, and high pulse rate. You'll soon forget to notice the negatives.

And sometimes, external information serves merely

to confirm that you <u>should</u> be miserable. I had a little thermometer hanging on my pack strap. One afternoon at Urraca Mesa, it read 92 degrees. One morning at Crooked Creek, it read 32 degrees. Both times it merely reinforced my inclination to be miserable. The information was not actionable. I packed it away deep in a side pocket and never looked at it again. The temperature was not controllable.

When things weren't going our way, we asked "How can we make this better?" and put our energies to work in a positive way.

We experienced bad food, cold, heat, blisters, split boots, tangled ropes, hurting knees, busted backpacks, wet tents, and a few bleeding wounds. And some <u>deeply</u> unsettling latrines. One boy took a long, quiet look at the latrine in Cathedral Rock campsite. He walked back to the group without comment, asked for the hand shovel, and headed out to find a sheltering shrub. I couldn't have been prouder.

This boy was one of our more unshakable Scouts, and I found myself wondering what had led him to admit defeat so quickly. I sauntered over to the latrine to assess the situation. It was a two-holer. The left position was covered with a large rock – not just any stone, but a three-inch-thick slab of natural limestone that was almost the exact size and shape of a toilet seat. I'd seen similar things in Flintstones episodes. Where it came from and how it got there was an enigma on par with Stonehenge. Grasping the mysticism of the structure, I left it unspoiled in its majesty.

I popped open the lid on the other position. I was confronted by human detritus that rose almost precisely level with the top of the seat frame. To this day, I am thankful that I was not wearing my eyeglasses, for a clearer vision of this spectacle may have doomed me to a lifetime of night-sweats and PTSD.

Not being spry enough to casually opt for the shovel-and-squat option, I had no choice but to violate the sanctity of the entombed position. Gathering strength, I lifted the fifty-pound stone cover on the sarcophagus and anxiously peered in like Howard Carter breeching King Tut's tomb. I discovered a treasure of comparable value: empty space. We were in business.

All challenges the boys encountered throughout the trek were met with similar clinical exploration of alternatives.

Not one member of the crew complained at any point in the back-country.

LESSON #4: Defeat and fatigue are 90% mental. Don't allow yourself to go there.

Sealed in stone.

5: Lift

All scout leaders have witnessed the gradual evolution of young scouts into early adulthood. Usually, this unfolds slowly over years. For one particular boy in our crew, I saw this transition in a period of two weeks at Philmont, and I found it to be my single most fulfilling experience as a leader.

When the trek started, "Trent" was reserved and a bit apart from the rest of the crew. He was the youngest member of the crew, and the only one not attending our local public school. One could tell that he was concerned that he might not fit in, and that he might not be up to the physical demands of the experience. The morning of our planned departure, he was sick, and I was concerned that he might not be ready for the rigors of day 1. However, after a few hours, he recovered enough that we managed a late departure.

With every day on the trail, I could see him changing. He worked hard at his assigned tasks, earning the respect of his older peers. And his self-confidence grew as he understood that the trek was challenging for *everyone*, and that we *all* were a bit intimidated by the tasks ahead of us.

On day three, we rolled into Crater Lake campsite.

The program theme was "logging camp". The highlight was something called spar pole climbing. The poles were basically fifty feet high stripped tree trunks planted vertically in the ground. The climb was effected using ankle gaffs and waist straps – the same basic gear that telephone linemen use to climb utility poles. Except that these trees were much more uneven, making it harder to get the gaffs firmly set and more likely for the strap to hang up on a limb stub when you're trying to work it up the pole.

It was scarier and more physically demanding than it looked from the ground. Other than the staffers, nobody scampered right up. More than anyone else, Trent struggled. About half way up, he stalled out.

The rest of the boys rallied behind him, yelling lots of encouragement and experimenting with various motivational incentives. They gravitated to the prospect of promising social outings with various movie starlets. Trial and error determined that "Megan Fox" and "Scarlett Johansen" produced the best results – either was good for a lunge of up to two vertical feet.

That did the trick and when he soon reached the top, a general celebration ensued. My turn was next, and I armed my son with my five favorite brands of Scotch whiskeys and craft beers in case I needed similar encouragement, but the need did not arise.

From that point onward, Trent was enthusiastically

embraced and encouraged by all. He opened up and became one of the more physically robust members of the crew, and he became a role model of quiet determination. And he started to have fun.

By the time we rolled into base camp ten days later, he had (like many of us) lost a few pounds, but had gained much _more_ than the rest of us in areas of self-confidence, determination, and camaraderie. And in the process, the rest of us gained tangible evidence of the true power of the Scouting program.

I sensed that the Philmont experience benefited Trent in a way that no other experience could have. The experience put renewed vigor into his determination to become an Eagle Scout, which he achieved two years later.

LESSON #5: Encouragement is stronger than gravity.

Spar pole climbing with gaffs & belt.

6: Darkness

Without the distractions of modern daily life, the rigor of the back-country leads one to focus on the basics: staying dry, keeping warm, and managing fatigue and aches. And food takes on a more important aspect.

Backpacking fare was not elegant. Most meals were comprised of high energy carbohydrates. Lunch might have a protein source like canned chicken or vacuum packed tuna accompanied by a few crackers and a couple of energy bars, most of which are composed of dried fruit and fiber. Some of these energy bars closely resembled bear scat in appearance, texture, and (we conjectured) taste. Dinner selections might include some kind of dehydrated fare like macaroni, eggs, or refried beans.

The food was plentiful and supported the clinical needs of an active hiker, but nobody would call it "satisfying". Eating a Philmont meal was a necessity, not a pleasure. A couple of the boys weren't eating all of their food – a situation that can cause problems at our sustained levels of physical activity. One of the other leaders attacked the problem like a mom trying to get her 1 year old to eat pureed green beans. He scored only modest success.

Early in the trek, occasional mention was made of "juicy cheeseburgers" at dinner time, but over time it became tacitly acknowledged that it was unproductive to dwell on the unattainable.

Some of the boys speculated how Jalapeno squeeze-cheese, one of our condiment staples, would taste on freshly roasted human flesh. As one of the larger and slower members of the crew, I slept poorly that night.

Some meals were augmented with "dessert selections" such as 6-packs of Nutter Butter or Oreo cookies. After a few days on the trail, these were like little treasures. One can imagine Oreos in the backcountry growing into a medium of exchange much like cigarettes in a prison.

Each staffed outpost had a box for crews to unload "un-needed food". Any crew could rifle through the box to upgrade their fare. Every time we opened the lids to hunt for treasures, we were inevitably disappointed to discover only items such as dried fruit chips, sunflower seed paste, dehydrated beans, and some of the more repugnant energy bars – all items reported to have been found untouched amongst the gnawed skeletons of the Donner Party.

Oreos were **NEVER** abandoned in these boxes.

Each Philmont meal comes sealed in pre-packaged, dual-portion bags. Many crews assign "food buddies" and they work out sharing of the load and meals. However, one of our crew was allergic to wheat, so he had his own food. We also tried to adhere to advice to not carry food and fuel/stoves in the same pack. This complicated food arrangements somewhat. So we randomly distributed food among packs to even out the weight. Since all food goes up in bear-bags each night, there was perpetual shuffling of these food allotments.

On day two, when we all sorted through the packs and piled up the bags for dinner, we came up short on Oreos. At first we thought it was a packaging mistake. To maintain the peace, I volunteered to go without that night.

This "cookie deficit" cropped up two more times in the next couple of days. Each time, I short-circuited the tension by volunteering to go without. Sometimes, more than one was missing. Something was clearly afoot. Only our compadre with gluten allergies was beyond suspicion, since he couldn't eat cookies.

Suspicion was focused on our picky eaters.

Nothing explicit was ever said about this issue, but you could feel it hanging over the crew like a black cloud. After a long day on the trail – often tired, hungry, and sometimes wet – it was never good news to be reminded that there was a scalawag amongst us. In the late afternoon shadows, I could look around the meal circle and see faces as hard-set and expressionless as royal sentries, but their eyes seemed to betray the dark thoughts of thieves and cannibals.

Food buddies were adopted from day five onward, pairs carried their own food, and the problem stopped.

LESSON #6: Character is illuminated by darkness & most revealed when nobody is looking.

Oreos: The currency of the back-country.

7: Solutions

Another of the "basics" that seemed to expand in prominence in the back-country was that most basic of bodily functions: the excretory system. Since we were an all-male crew, urination was relatively spontaneous, and involved the nearest tree. In fact, Philmont <u>discourages</u> urination in the latrines.

That's a welcome thing, because the latrines were not generally pleasant places for relaxed retreat. The best were relatively conventional outhouses with two doors and private seating. A prior generation of latrines were two-holers where you could rub knees with a neighbor. I often contemplated what the proper protocol was for the second arrival at one of these facilities – a demur exit to wait outside, or settling into the vacant position with swagger and extroversion, trying to avoid unpleasant jabs and vistas as either party proceeded to the paperwork phase. The situation never materialized, and so the mystery remains.

The oldest latrines were essentially coffin-like boxes in the open with a toilet lid on each end. The standard training included a careful inspection of the apparatus for cobwebs, insects or worse before settling in. This involved a stick, preferably one that had not been similarly employed by a prior occupant. All modesty was lost during these times. On the upside, the views from these thrones were sometimes exhilarating and more than made up for the threat of splinters and the lack of proper reading materials. And conversation came more easily when second tenants did not occupy your direct field of vision.

At each food replenishment depot, a crew was generally provided with three or four rolls of toilet paper. These rolls were as carefully protected as the food and stoves. A hard rain on unprotected rolls could wipe out the wipes. In camp, a roll in a zip-lock bag was always available under the dining fly to prevent the need to search through backpacks for a roll when the urge struck.

One member of our crew seemed to develop an urgent need to visit the latrine only after everyone else was loaded up and ready to set out on the morning trail. After a few days, we all sort of "built in" a fake departure to trigger this ritual.

There were 4 factors that tended to disrupt even the most well-regulated bowel habits:

>1) We were encouraged to drink massive amounts of water to prevent dehydration on the trail. "Clear & copious" urination was a requirement. A gallon or more per day of water consumption was not uncommon.
>2) The energy bars were <u>loaded</u> with bran and oats, providing a liberal daily dose of fiber.
>3) In order to carry the backpack load on one's hips, the waist belt must be TIGHT. It was like

wearing a large boa constrictor around your waist all day.

4) We were drinking water from streams, doing our best to treat it with purification tablets, but the threat of diarrhea was omnipresent.

As the days progressed and the crew moved further each day, we also tended to have more frequent "movements" as well. When we rolled into Beaubien camp on day four, every member of the crew was eager to visit the "Red Roof Inn" privy at our campsite. We went through two rolls of toilet paper in a couple of hours.

I referred to this phenomenon as our "Troop Surge". We had a significant increase in our presence on the ground, so to speak.

The result was that when we rolled up to the supply depot on our 5th morning to replenish our empty backpacks, we were down to only about a dozen squares of toilet paper.

We stepped up to the supply window and loaded up with 24 bags of food. We topped off the stoves with 2 pints of fuel. There was no toilet paper on the counter. I laughed a bit and said that we'd be needing at least four or five rolls.

Only a midnight knock from an Army Chaplain could have delivered worse news: "No can do. We're out."

You have to appreciate the situation: This was the only civilized outpost for miles. The next supply depot was four days and 35 miles away. This was a **HUGE** problem.

I immediately considered the obvious course of action – working out an exchange of Oreos for toilet paper. However, since they were already presiding over a small warehouse of foodstuffs, the prospect of bribing these guys with a few crumbly packets of Oreos seemed to carry the same prospect of success as discretely sliding a couple of gold coins across the Commandant's desk at Fort Knox. So capitalism was quickly abandoned for other strategies.

I begged. I groveled. I gave an impassioned speech about the "help other people at all times" provision of the Scout Oath. I attempted bribery. And I got ****ONE**** roll of toilet paper. Nothing else was to be forthcoming. They were really out, and none was expected until the next day, when we'd be long gone. I took our single roll and sat down on the step of the porch. It began to rain and hail vigorously.

It is an oversight by Noah Webster that my picture does not appear next to the definition of "equanimity". I am by nature a bit of a stoic. Over the course of my life, I cannot recall ever having been approached by anyone proclaiming "Well, you're certainly effusive today!" Neither am I a "Debbie Downer". Being an engineer by training and disposition, it has never been an issue of whether the glass is half full or half empty – it is simply a matter of the glass being twice as big as it <u>needs</u> to be.

So I began to study the wrapper on that roll of toilet paper with the same intense intellectual fatality I bring to income tax preparation. It clearly stated that there were 240 sheets on that roll. I worked through the math: 12 people with 4 days to our next supply station worked out to five sheets per person per day. Wow. At least it was good two-ply product.

A grim resolve took hold in my heart: although I was willing to sacrifice my <u>Oreos</u> to maintain the working relationship of the crew, I'd be ***damned*** if some bottom-feeder scumbag was going to purloin a single square of my god-given <u>toilet paper</u> allotment in the dark of night. I was simply NOT going to let this roll out of my sight for the next four days. I reflected on Ebenezer Scrooge greedily counting his gold coins by candlelight each evening, and I found no fault with his audit practices.

As the hail fell and the sky (and my disposition) darkened, I tried to impart the seriousness of the situation to the boys, but I wasn't getting through. It became clear to me that, much like the horrors of mortal combat, until the realities of the toilet paper situation were actually experienced first-hand, there was no way to overcome the swaggering bravado that is the natural territory of the young.

As I was pondering the hail and sliding deeper into

depression on the porch, the other two leaders were taking shelter in the modest general store at this outpost, exploring the selection of embroidered patches for sale. Making idle conversation with the proprietor, they discovered that a sales contest was in full blossom between the six resupply depots, and that this outpost needed only to sell one more complete set of patches to win the contest. Russ and Rich, familiar with our dilemma, dangled the prospect of a $50 patch set purchase in return for two rolls of toilet paper from the clerk's personal stash. The deal was closed.

They emerged from the store with twelve patches and two rolls. Never before or since has the market price of toilet paper been so high, yet the buyers emerged from the transaction with smug satisfaction of an advantageous bargain cleverly attained. Economics professors may get much mileage from this clinical study in supply and demand relationships, but the real lesson was a bit more human in nature: the sellers valued the prospect of public sales-contest recognition more than either direct financial gain or the quiet personal satisfaction of a charitable act.

As it turned out, three rolls were more than enough to last the next four days. Little did we know at the time that after the Troop Surge at Beaubien, we were as cleaned out as a Political Action Committee in late November. If we had swallowed a Brussels sprout whole, it would have dropped to the ground un-scuffed within twenty minutes. The Troop Surge was over, and demand for toilet paper dropped off precipitously.

LESSON #7: When the system games you, you game the system. Look for the win/win.

More valuable than Oreos?

8: Beauty

Many books about the Appalachian Trail comment on the treacherous rockiness of the pathway in Pennsylvania. One book apologized for the lack of commentary about scenic overlooks along the trails around Allentown, observing that "we were too busy looking at our feet to make note of the scenery".

The same danger exists at Philmont. The trails are tough and sometimes rocky, and there can at times be a grim determination to reach the next camp in time to participate in the program-du-jour. We were in such a situation after cresting Mount Phillips. One of our crew was under the weather, and a potential storm was closing in on our position along an exposed Thunder Ridge at an altitude of 11,000 feet. We were focused on making time before the lightning arrived.

Suddenly a call came from the back of the trail line: "Stop. Everyone turn around." We all wheeled expecting to see a bear, an injury, or some piece of failed equipment.

Workers on the upper floors of tall office buildings sometimes enjoy morning vistas when only the highest buildings protrude from a thick blanket of ground fog. Something similar was afoot here.

We all witnessed one of the most beautiful sights I

have ever seen. Two layers of clouds extended for a couple of miles to the east. About 1000 feet below us, the mountain valleys were socked in by a thick blanket of gray clouds, probably delivering rain to the lower altitudes. About 300 feet over our heads was a similar stratum of dense, gray clouds. In the slit between these two expansive horizontal layers, we could look eastward for miles to the bright, sunlit Great Plains and the town of Cimarron. It was a golden view of unspoiled paradise through a horizontal slit in a thick concrete wall. We all gaped for about thirty seconds, at which time the upper layer of clouds dropped to our level and cut off the view.

At that time, I resolved to take more care to notice the beauty of Philmont. Among my top candidates:

The meadow from the cabin porch at Crooked Creek. Perched on a hill beneath the largest Ponderosa pine I've ever seen, this log cabin overlooked a grassy valley with a few donkeys and a meandering steam toward a far hillside of aspen trees. I'd gladly retrace the 20 miles of trail hell to get a glimpse of this valley when the aspens turn yellow in October.

Crater Lake campfire against the backdrop of the Tooth of Time. The campfire area at Crater Lake perches on a cliff edge facing north across a deep valley to the Tooth of Time and Grizzly Tooth. As we listened to some of the best live bluegrass music in the state, the last bit of sunshine worked its way up the Tooth as the sun set over the high mountains to the west. The sparks from the campfire rose to infinity, merging with the limitless stars in the sky.

<u>Bison in our camp at Cathedral Rock.</u> We were busy setting up camp and trying to keep an eye out for a bear reported to be in the area. Suddenly, somebody pointed to a giant bison standing about 75 yards away. It was huge and radiated raw power. It was probably potentially more dangerous than any bear. We silently stared at each other for five minutes and then it meandered along.

<u>Livestock pasture at Beaubien.</u> This camp sat on the side of a great open meadow between two forested ridges. A herd of cattle grazed in the valley, and a horse stockade sat on the far side of the meadow. A meandering stream bisected the meadow. It was a classic ranch setting, like something out of a John Ford western movie.

<u>The staffer at Crooked Creek.</u> A gal in her early 20s was one of the ersatz "homesteaders" at Crooked Creek. As she made candles at a fire, she spoke to me of her daily chores that included feeding and brushing the livestock, milking the cow, and retrieving water from the distant spring. Every Wednesday, she led the donkeys several miles to Phillips Junction to get supplies for the cabin. She obviously enjoyed the simplicity and remoteness of Crooked Creek, the camaraderie of the small staff, and cooking meals on the wood stove. She spoke matter-of-factly of her fifteen mile walk over

three mountains to get back to base camp for her occasional weekend off.

Unlike most young adults, she spoke in a manner that conveyed deep self-confidence and comfortable wisdom. It suddenly hit me: she wasn't speaking "in-character" – she had actually <u>become</u> the homesteader. This was clearly someone who thrived in the setting. Like Henry David Thoreau, she had sought out her cabin in the woods, adopted a life of simplicity, and was finding herself. I found myself making comparisons to my desk job in a big city, and I was deeply envious.

<u>The view north from Tooth Ridge trail.</u> This trail went on for miles on the crest of a rocky, largely treeless ridge. The plains to the east bled up into a bucolic valley to the majesty of Cathedral Rock and the shimmering reservoir at its base.

<u>Sunrise from Tooth Ridge.</u> More on this later.

There were many others. As I reflect on this list, two thoughts occur to me.

The first was that as I later looked over the photographs from our trek, I was struck by how poorly the photos captured this beauty. Ansel Adams we were not. The framing was either too wide or too narrow, or the light was not quite bright enough, or the dynamics of the setting were lost in the static frame. The true beauty that I remembered wasn't just a <u>visual</u> snapshot – it was a moment in the context of the day and place.

    The other realization is that beauty is best when you aren't looking for it. It has to be unexpected. Pulling off the road at a signed "scenic overlook" is never as awe-inspiring as when you round a curve and stumble into the same vista.

    I owe a great debt to whoever shouted "Stop. Everyone turn around."

LESSON #8: Beauty is all around us. Remember to notice.

One of many scenic mountain meadows.

9: Difficulty

Mountains show up as allegory in many Eagle Scout Courts of Honor. There is a reason for that.

Nothing frames a challenge quite like the visible crest of a distant, high mountain. And Philmont is chock-a-block full of mountains. Just looking at the topo maps back in New Jersey, Philmont's mountains intimidated me. It was a function of oxygen, load, height, and frequency.

I have lived at an altitude of 200 feet above sea level for many years. A "tall mountain" in New Jersey is 1600 feet above sea level - rigorous to climb, but doable in a bit over an hour.

Several years ago, I drove straight through from the Denver airport to the top of Trail Ridge Road in Rocky Mountain National Park. I got out of the car at 12,000 feet to walk 100 yards up a slight incline to a lookout. I've never been so out of breath in my life. I had flashbacks to this moment as I looked at the 11,800 altitude stamped on the map for Mount Phillips. We were going to tackle that puppy with full packs. Who picked that trek, anyway?

I spent some time on the bike and treadmill in the weeks approaching our departure. But during our brief stopover in Colorado Springs, even a brisk walk still led to heavy breathing. I was expecting the worst. And it came.

The night before departure, our crew dumped our packs and challenged the utility of every item. We jettisoned several knives, some rope, and a few pots. Then we re-packed and weighed packs, which ranged from 40 pounds to 60 pounds.

We had a lot of smallish boys in our crew. There was a bias toward shifting the load to adults and some of the larger boys. Despite that, we had boys carrying a little less than half their body weight in their packs. These boys shouldered the weight with the nonchalance of carpenter ants.

My pack weighed in at 62 pounds on the morning of our departure. It set well, but it was definitely mighty heavy. At eight pounds per gallon, water was a non-trivial portion of the load, one that promised to increase a lot on days when we were to be far away from water supplies.

Normally, the first couple of days in the back-country are less rigorous routes to condition the crew for the later part of the trek. Our day 1 was like that, with a couple of modest climbs to blow the cobwebs out of our lungs. It was invigorating.

Day two featured a steep 1200 foot climb from the valley to the top of Urraca Mesa. It was hard. Day three started with a climb up the backside of Urraca that was even harder. And the day four climb from Crater Lake over Fowler Pass at 9300 feet was an absolute killer. I contemplated sawing off my left arm to reduce my load by seven pounds and made a mental note to pack a third lung next time I come to Philmont.

At about this time, knees, hips, and muscles were not yet inured to a hard day's climbing. Things hurt, but we were steadily building up strength.

We spent the next three days at 9000+ feet, and we were all acclimated to the altitude as we approached Mount Phillips. We were heavily loaded with extra food & water when we departed for Mount Phillips. The trail was the steepest we encountered, and roughly equal protests were registered by our legs and lungs as we proceeded up the stair-like path.

Topping this mountain at around noontime was a major accomplishment for us all. At the time, we thought this was the biggest challenge that would face us on this trek. We had seen it coming for days, and we'd been steadily closing in on it in terms of both distance and altitude. This was a large and obvious pinnacle that we had measured our progress toward.

We happily set off down the other side of the mountain with a huge sense of achievement, secure in our confidence that we could tackle any geology plopped in our pathway.

Little did we know that the true test was still two days ahead of us – the segment from Cathedral Rock to Tooth Ridge Camp. This was also an "extra water" segment, but it was much longer than our prior trek over Mount Phillips. It started easy but changed to a very steep 2000 foot climb for several hours up to Tooth Ridge. Lunch at the top was welcome and late. Little did we know what lay before us: a winding, boulder-strewn, interminable slog along the exposed apex of Tooth Ridge. For once our lungs weren't the limiting factor – it was raw stamina. The constant stepping up and down from large boulders with the heavy packs was physically exhausting and murder on already frayed knees.

Every emergence from behind a rock pile or a blind switchback revealed – yet another rock pile or set of switchbacks. Our ultimate destination remained obscured in the unknown distance. There were no markers of progress, and it simply seemed like there was no prospect that the journey would ever end.

Finally, at five o'clock, we rolled into Tooth Ridge after nine full hours of hiking. We simply collapsed, now confident that we had <u>really</u> tested our true limits of endurance. At this point, we knew that there wasn't anything that Philmont could throw at us that we couldn't tackle.

Reflecting on my first day at base camp, it now became clear to me what had so battered those crews coming into camp down the Ridge Trail. It hadn't been Mount Phillips or Baldy Mountain with their prominent summits and shouts of celebration. It was the grinding torture and uncertainty of Tooth Ridge that was the ultimate test that they had proudly overcome.

Such is daily life. We always relish the reaching of bite-sized milestones, but the most heroic achievements are the long slogs – the three year journey to Eagle Scout and the eighteen years to bring a newborn to the first day of college.

LESSON #9: Some mountains are tall. The hardest ones are the long ones with uncertain conclusions.

The endless rocky trail along Tooth Ridge

10: Milestones

When I think of Philmont, I mostly remember the rigor of the climbs, gasping for breath and trying to think of something in my pack that I didn't really need to carry up that hill. The best part of every hill was the top.

Coming up the back side of Urraca Mesa was a really steep challenge on day 2. I was dragging badly, and a few of the boys seemed to be more concerned about me than I was. When I finally crested the top edge of the plateau, I spontaneously turned about and said "Take <u>that</u> you SOB." (I paraphrase a bit, perhaps.) I needed the official statement of victory, a ceremonial notch on the rifle stock if you will.

The notion seemed to take hold a bit. From that point onward, whenever we crested a particularly vexing summit, somebody would shout out "Take that you SOB." The chorus was loudest atop Mount Phillips.

Every successful camp set-up and tear down had its moments of satisfaction.

We were on the trail on July 4. We had struggled over a high pass and had just emerged from a tree line into an open valley with a stream, a huge vista, and a big herd of cattle. Suddenly, from the other side of the valley, we heard a rousing rendition of the Star Spangled Banner. We could barely discern the other crew. We applauded loudly when they finished. It remains one of my favorite Fourth of July celebrations ever.

Day 5 was a "work day" at Beaubien. The blue pine bark beetle has wreaked havoc on a large fraction of the trees in Philmont. It was the first time I had seen direct evidence of the kind of environmental damage that an invasive species can have on an established ecosystem, and it was unsettling. Anyway, the camp staff wanted to thin out the standing deadwood to control fire risk at this major outpost. So we were all armed with goggles, hardhats, and saws and directed to cut down any standing dead tree.

We had a great time. There's something about watching a tall tree fall that is awesome – it sort of draws attention to the miracle of how it got there in the first place. We felled scores of trees and cut them up into firewood. The sense of satisfaction was palpable. Not a soul complained about all the hard work we signed up for that morning.

But when I reflect back on celebration and satisfaction at Philmont, nothing can beat the basics: a hamburger and fries at Heck's Restaurant in Cimarron the day we walked back into camp. To be clean and eating "regular" food again was irrefutable evidence that we were done. Although we had another 36 hours of packing and travel ahead of us, that lunch at Heck's was the real end of the Philmont experience.

Philmont was a collection of hundreds of challenges. Its power involves building the realization that you're up to them all. Celebrating is a key part of tackling each challenge.

Much like the guy who shouted "Stop! Everyone turn around!" when he saw a scene of great beauty, we also need folks who remember to shout out "Stop! We have achieved something meaningful." Celebration is the cement that builds self-confidence.

LESSON #10: Celebrate when you can.

11: Prepare

I found the prospect of Philmont at age 52 to be very intimidating. And I suspect that I wasn't alone amongst my crewmates. It would be the most physically challenging experience of my life. I knew next to nothing about backpacking through the wilderness. But I knew people who had done this before, and who were willing to share their lessons.

First of all, about a year ahead of our departure date, we formed our crew and made a public commitment to follow through on the experience. We were "signed up" from this point forward.

Second, we studied up on the topics we would need to know. We publicly acknowledged our ignorance. Then we invited veterans of the experience to come talk to us. From these presentations and the council website videos and guides, we learned a tremendous amount about what was ahead of us. Many of us took Wilderness First Aid, CPR, and on-line scout training classes to ensure that we had the required certifications. We had the theory and the facts in our HEADS at that point. That was achieved through study.

Then we had to move the knowledge to our HANDS. This was achieved through practice. We outfitted ourselves with the lightest gear we could find. We winnowed down our stuff to the barest essentials. We went on practice hikes. We ran through drills on camp set up and tear down. We cooked some official Philmont dinners, and we learned to string bear-bags up into the trees. We loaded up packs and wrestled them along trails. Now we knew that we could actually do the tasks. In the rain and in the dark.

By working together as a cohesive unit and assigning specific roles, we became an interdependent team. We trusted each other's skills and follow-through. We knew that when we were out of cell phone range and couldn't call for help from others, we would be prepared to help each other. We had built <u>trust</u>. We had the resolve to tackle this task. Our <u>HEARTS</u> were now ready.

At this point we knew we were as ready as anyone can be. When the unexpected arose on the trek, we had a pretty good idea of what to do. It was hard to think of anything other than an unfortunate injury that could prevent us all from walking back into base camp on Day 12. And that's what we did, probably with less wear, tear, and friction than most crews that summer.

Sure, some crews just "show up and wing it". Most of them make it through to the other side. But they spend a lot more energy focused on getting through the basics, and there's a lot more friction as the learning experiments and inevitable failures occur in a higher risk setting. These crews don't learn the same lessons that our crew did.

We will all face many other intimidating challenges in our lives: going away to college, starting our first job, moving to a distant city, giving that first big speech in front of hundreds of people, and even raising children. Many of these young men will use the same steps outlined above to approach those challenges as well, and they will be more successful for it.

Will Philmont be as uplifting for me the second time? Probably not, because now I <u>know</u> I can do it. But I bet I'll learn a completely different set of lessons next time.

<u>LESSON #11: Self confidence comes from converting ignorance & fear into knowledge & experience. Learn the process: head to hands to heart.</u>

A fistful of training certifications.

12: Risk

"Mortality" is a concept that doesn't really take root in the human psyche until after the age of 25. Military recruiting, competitive downhill skiing, and the motorcycle industry owe their very existences to this axiom. Teenage boys regularly demonstrate a deep understanding of this fact by seizing almost ANY opportunity to prove their immortality by enthusiastically inserting themselves into the middle of any number of high risk situations. Philmont is a graduate-level laboratory in this regard.

Taking a quick look at the leading causes of accidental death in America, many of the top contenders can be almost completely disregarded within the confines of Philmont: motor vehicle accidents, electrocution, and violent crime come quickly to mind.

And despite all the stories about Philmont trail food, I also feel comfortable eliminating "poisoning" from the list.

But a huge number of very low-odds hazards that are almost unthinkable in normal daily life suddenly become very real prospects at Philmont: animal bite/sting/mauling, lightning strikes, flash floods, falling trees, heatstroke, hypothermia, dehydration, over-exertion, dysentery, and falls of over 100 feet.

And like any organization with a vibrant legal department, the Boy Scouts of America do everything possible to make the prospect of these events as intimidating as possible (to decrease the odds of occurrence) and TRAIN, TRAIN, TRAIN to make sure that if they DO actually occur, the consequences are rapidly and correctly addressed.

Many leaders and older scouts participate in countless classes prior to setting foot on the property: CPR, Wilderness First Aid, water purification, and lightning management to name a few. A fistful of American Red Cross certification cards are an essential part of a full backpack.

All of this serves to scare the hell out of the leaders and to heighten the attraction of the place to the scouts, almost to a level of euphoric hysteria.

Some of the most beautiful vistas on earth are from the abrupt edges of mountainous precipices, and Phimont is chock-a-block full of them. Through repeated experimentation, we proved that it is impossible to keep teens from flocking to every unstable cliff on the property. We settled for asking them to remove backpacks and hold down the horseplay around cliffs.

"Animal issues" are the least familiar risks to most of us, yet Scouts are drawn to wild animals like lawyers to ambulances. Despite hourly pleas to behave otherwise, every time we heard some distant voice scream "BEAR!"

the crew would immediately split, with the boys running <u>toward</u> the yell and the leaders <u>stepping back</u>. We were fortunate in having few close encounters.

During our stay, reports circulated that a burly, veteran ranger at one of the camps awoke to frantic bleating from his pet goat tied outside the cabin. He reportedly ran out, found a black bear attacking his goat, and cold-cocked it with a right uppercut. Having dealt with a statistically valid sample size of these rangers, I believed the report.

During my darkest hour in that hailstorm, I recall seeking solace by reminding myself that rattlesnakes have an aversion to altitudes above 8000 feet, so I was beyond the reach of at least one potential misery. (Like much of the dubious lore that had been passed to me by grizzled leaders, this was, when I returned to civilization, actually corroborated by Google and Wikipedia searches.) At almost that very moment, a couple of mule deer wandered by the campsite. They took one look at our forlorn crew and quickly moved on to a more positive environment.

At Clear Creek, there were reports of a mountain lion lurking on the trail to the top of Mount Phillips. I had disturbing dreams that night about serial disappearances of straggling members of our pack line, sort of like bad scenes from the "Predator" movies.

Our most noteworthy wild animal encounter was in

camp on one of the last evenings. A boy had spurned the privy, and was doing his business over a cat-hole behind a bush in the distance. We watched a huge bison slowly wander out of the woods toward this bush, approaching the distracted scout from behind. The beast snorted about 50 feet behind the boy, who earned the enmity of government bureaucrats world-wide by completely omitting the paperwork phase of his task. (We went back later in the evening to retrieve the indispensable shovel and toilet paper.)

We were attacked repeatedly by the most pernicious predator on the premises, the common chipmunk. They chewed into unattended backpacks during rest stops. For a while, I took some comfort in rationalizing them as the likely cause of our missing Oreos. That may have been a reach.

The least glamorous health risk is "bad water". Rigorous enforcement of water purification at the back-country camps required constant reminding. Despite the obvious issues of dehydration, discomfort, and widely-spaced latrines, the tight toilet paper rations can make an outbreak of dysentery a particularly unpleasant downer to a nice walk in the woods. Fortunately, as more wells are drilled at key camps, this risk seems to be declining.

"Drug overdose" is a top cause of accidental death in America. On first blush, this would seem to be another risk to casually dismiss within the confines of Philmont, and it certainly is for the boys. However, as Tylenol and Advil became an important "fifth food group" for us adults, we found ourselves playing fast and loose with the recommended maximum dosage guidelines. We approached the edge of this precipice but did not fall.

All the firearms on site were closely managed by counselors, and they remained pointed in the correct directions at all times.

So as it turned out, we were afflicted by no health risks more serious than blisters, aching knees, tired backs, and fatigue. Our crew was fortunate in this regard.

Every adult leader taking a crew of scouts to Philmont has the same unspoken goal at the top of his list: Bring back the same number of boys you left with, even if they are in less-than-perfect condition. After sitting through the countless hours of training and after a couple of days on the trail, it becomes gnawingly clear that this isn't the slam-dunk that it appeared to be when you signed up.

Only the father of a newborn can fully identify with the constant, gnawing worry that hangs over a leader on every step across the reservation.

LESSON #12: Having a pulse is a necessary pre-requisite for having a good time. But a life without risk is an empty existence.

The most subtle, pernicious predator at Philmont prepares to attack.

Life on the edge.

13: Luck

Confidence is built by successfully dealing with difficult situations. Usually, these recoveries were catalyzed by good preparation and training, or by improvising clever solutions as unexpected events arose. No crew should set foot on the property without 100 feet of parachute cord and a half roll of duct tape.

When all else fails, good luck can be a savior. I can think of 3 instances where situations that could have wrecked an otherwise stellar outdoor experience were solved by the divine intervention of God.

One of the smallest boys in our crew did not care for Philmont cuisine. He routinely and surreptitiously flung his food into the bushes most evenings. He became unable to carry his load after we crested Mount Phillips. The other boys quietly re-distributed his burden amongst themselves, and he barely made it to the next camp, a waterless clearing far away from the emergency access roads.

We hoped it was altitude sickness, and that the remedy of "retreat 1000 feet" would help. But he did not improve after an hour of rest.

As the leaders conferred on the best means of getting the afflicted boy to a manned campsite, he decided that maybe eating a square meal was indeed a necessity. He ate a large meal and turned in early. The next morning, he was good to go and finished the trek. I don't know what voice drove him to eat, but I'm thankful for it.

On the last night in the back-country, we were camping at Tooth Ridge. At that site, it is something of a tradition to rise early and backtrack a few miles to watch sunrise from the Tooth of Time outcropping. A very emotional schism formed in our crew, with about half the boys wanting to hurry to base camp early so we could go into Cimarron for a civilized lunch. The other half wanted to backtrack to the Tooth for sunrise. At the end of a protracted debate, the "head to base camp" position won out by a single vote. This put half the crew into a horrible funk, threatening to end an otherwise stellar outing on a downer.

We rose at 4:30, broke camp in the dark, and headed away from the Tooth toward base camp. As it happened, just about the time the sky started to brighten, we encountered another outcropping of rock that overlooked the plains below. We sat down to have a grumpy breakfast.

As the dawn steadily progressed, we found ourselves perfectly positioned to witness the most awe-inspiring spectacle of the week. Light, wispy clouds formed high in the sky over the plains. As the sun rose, they changed from gray to deep purple to bright blue to orange and then a fiery yellow. Almost on cue, the sun peeked out over the edge of the prairie, seemingly hundreds of miles to the east. The base camp glowed as a golden Mecca at the base of the mountain ridge. Every camera in the crew was in use. We sat there for a full hour, and all agreed that there was NO WAY that the view from the Tooth could have compared favorably. Everyone was happy again.

We set off for base camp. A few hours later, we celebrated a return to civilization under the "welcome back" portal, and we were first in line for equipment check in. After a quick shower, we took the bus into town and got the front table at the best eatery in town.

You may think that kind of good luck would be hard to beat. But wait there's more!

Reflect back to our cold, smoky campfire in the hailstorm. The boys were nearing fisticuffs over assessing the blame for the tangled bear-bag ropes high up in the forest canopy. My disposition was approaching the nadir of my life.

Suddenly we heard deep masculine voices approaching our campsite. In walked a half dozen burly young men carrying chainsaws, axes, and gas cans. They were Philmont's equivalent of Navy Seals - a "clearing crew" that was in the area downing deadwood to prevent forest fires.

Our first revelations were that perhaps <u>our</u> loaded backpacks were almost buoyant compared to <u>their</u>

loads. And then we noticed that several of them were lugging climbing gaffs.

After a little polite, patient conversation expressing our admiration for the rigor of their assigned duties, they asked us how our trek was proceeding. We obliquely worked the conversation around to our dilemma involving the tangled ropes. One of the guys peered heavenward into the forest canopy, confidently stated "no problem", donned his climbing gaffs, and scrambled high up the offending trees. He required no encouraging shouts referencing Hollywood starlets or Scotch whiskey. The untangled ropes landed at our feet.

The misty origins of Greek mythology tales had become evident. If they had somehow restored our missing Oreos as an encore, we would have no doubt erected some kind of temple on the site.

That completely turned the tide of events. As if that wasn't enough of a sign from heaven, the hail stopped, the sun came out, and a ranger arrived to tell us that an opening had materialized at the black powder rifle range.

The fire even started to produce heat.

LESSON #13: Sometimes, things just work out.

An unexpected sunrise vista from Tooth Ridge

Coda

Many books and lists have been written about what to bring to Philmont. This is not one of those. This book is about what to take away.

So, why was I shivering around that smoky, stingy fire in July? Indeed, why would <u>any</u> sane fifty-something adult elect to wander around for two weeks with a bunch of hyperactive boys, beyond the reach of hygiene and comfort, out of breath and overloaded? To seek. By discarding all but the most Neolithic layers of existence, one may jettison the distractions of modernity, and rediscover the principles and joys of life at the atomic level.

Why 13 lessons? Simply because after much reflection (catalyzed by time, cigars, and the occasional glass of Scotch whiskey) that's how many there were.

The boys kept simple journals of their Philmont experiences as a Backpacking merit badge requirement. As I flipped through their notepads in subsequent weeks, I could discern shimmers of similar gestating revelations lurking in many of their jottings. I find myself hoping that they too have since crystallized lessons that will resurface at important times later in their lives. Scouting is an environment that tends to do that.

I went to Philmont in 2010. This is what I took away.

But I also left something behind. Someday, preferably when the aspens are bright yellow in late September, I'll get the opportunity to go back and find it again.

A rite of passage: hanging up the boots after a long journey.

In Brief Praise of Scouting

As my children progressed through college and toward employment, they often commented on how admissions officers and corporate recruiters valued the appearance of "Eagle Scout" on a resume or application. These two words convey more than any clever 2-page essay or thirty-minute job interview. Those who know what "Philmont" means will place almost as much value on that entry.

Scouts have learned that teamwork, knowledge, preparation, and determination can overcome almost any challenge – rappelling, sailing the ocean, hiking the High Rockies. Even the dreaded Eagle Scout Project. Tackling these challenges builds self-confidence.

They've learned that when you're out of cell phone range, you can call upon yourself and your teammates.

They've learned that action is a more powerful tool to effect change than complaining.

They've learned that some goals take a long time to achieve, and that even the most intimidating goals in life can be digested one bite at a time.

They've learned and practiced a moral code to live by: The Scout Law. Some may think it's hokey, but I can't think of a better list of twelve words against which to measure oneself.

Competence. Confidence. Perseverance. Integrity. These are attributes that we associate with maturity. Long slogs like the Trail to Eagle and Philmont are the forges of these characteristics. I have been very fortunate to have been able to assist a number of young men along these journeys.

A special thanks to the 10 boys and 2 adults from Troop 90 who took me along on this wonderful journey. And to the High Adventure staff of the Patriot's Path Council who prepared us to get the most from this experience.

Made in the USA
Monee, IL
11 December 2021